P9-DGG-118

SLAP, SQUEAK & SCATTER

HOW ANIMALS COMMUNICATE

STEVE JENKINS

HOUGHTON MIFFLIN COMPANY

BOSTON 2001

Animals, like people, have important things to tell one another. They may need to warn of approaching danger or let others in their group know where to find food. They may want to protect their territory, keep their family together, or find a mate. Sending and receiving these kinds of messages is called communication.

Animals send messages with sounds, visual signals, and touch. They use odors and chemical messages, create vibrations in the ground, or even light up to communicate with others of their kind. Learning how animals communicate helps us understand how they live and why they do some of the unusual things they do.

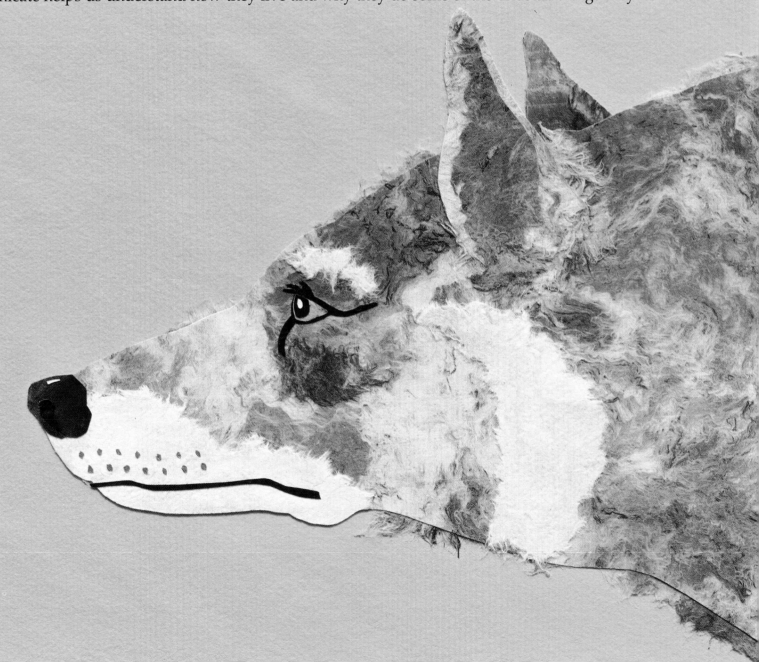

Many animals communicate to warn one another of danger. When every member of a group watches out for predators, they are all more likely to survive.

A beaver that detects danger will warn other beavers by slapping its tail on the water with such force that the sound can be heard half a mile away.

Vervet monkeys use warning cries to alert other monkeys in their group of danger. They have different cries for eagles, leopards, and snakes. If the eagle alarm is given, the monkeys dive under a bush. The leopard alarm makes them rush to the top of a tree. If they hear the snake alarm, the monkeys grab their young, stand up on their hind legs, and look around to locate the danger.

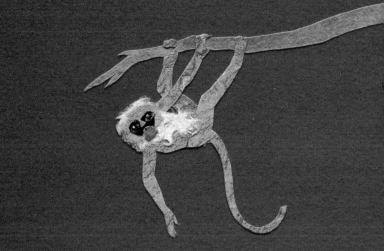

When it runs away from danger, the white-tailed deer alerts other deer by raising its tail and revealing a patch of white fur underneath.

The chaffinch has three different songs, including
one that says "a predator is near." Another says "I'm
injured," and a third song tells other chaffinches
"I'm getting ready to fly."

Communication can help one animal tell another that it just wants to be friends, that it accepts the other as leader, or to just stay away. These messages help avoid conflict or fights that could cause serious injury.

The mole rat lives a solitary life — it doesn't get along well with other mole rats. It avoids underground fights by banging its head on the roof of its tunnel to let others know it's coming.

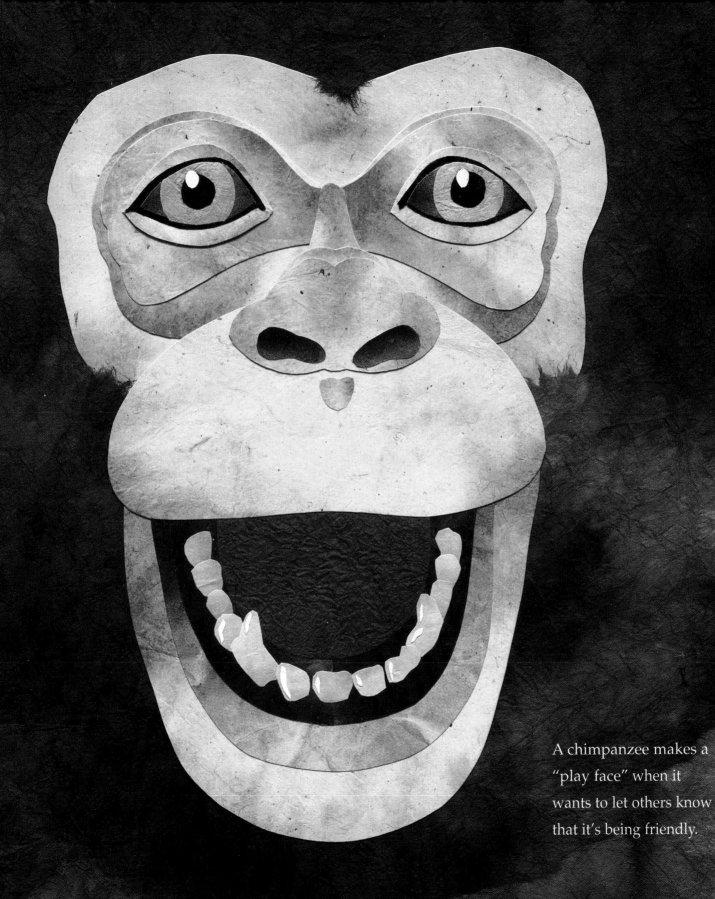

A chimpanzee makes a "play face" when it wants to let others know that it's being friendly.

Rather than risk a fight
in which one of them
could be hurt, a wolf
will lower its body to
the ground and flatten
its ears to show that it
submits to a stronger
wolf.

For most animals to reproduce, they must to be able to find a mate. To do this, they've developed many different ways of communicating with the opposite sex.

When he's looking for a female toad, the male barking tree toad inflates a sac in his throat that can be blown up like a balloon. This sac vibrates and makes his croak louder. The sound attracts female toads who are also looking for a mate.

Grasshoppers, like many other insects, make sounds
to attract a mate by rubbing their legs together.
They have a series of pegs on their hind legs, which
they rub on the edge of their wings to produce
a loud call. Each species of grasshopper has a
different number and pattern of pegs to produce a
different sound.

Blue-footed boobies perform a special mating dance. They show off their bright blue feet to potential mates by stepping from foot to foot, pointing to the sky with their bills, and lifting their tails. Boobies are very territorial. They normally attack other boobies that enter their nesting space. Their complex dance allows them to get used to their mates and overcome their natural defensiveness.

When a male orb-web spider approaches a female to mate, he plucks her web in a special rhythm so she won't think he's her trapped prey and eat him. This is a dangerous time for the male, who is much smaller than the female — sometimes she ignores his message and kills him.

The male humpback whale often sings to attract a mate. The whale's songs, which are up to thirty minutes long, are performed for hours at a time. Other whales can hear the songs from hundreds of miles away.

Animals communicate with one another to keep their group together, to find their offspring, or to ask for help.

When ring-tailed lemurs move through tall grass or brush, they carry their striped tails high in the air. Their tails act as flags that help their group keep track of one another.

Dolphins use lots of different sounds to speak to one another. When a dolphin is injured or sick, it makes a whistling sound that calls other dolphins to its aid. They help the hurt or sick dolphin to the surface so it can breathe.

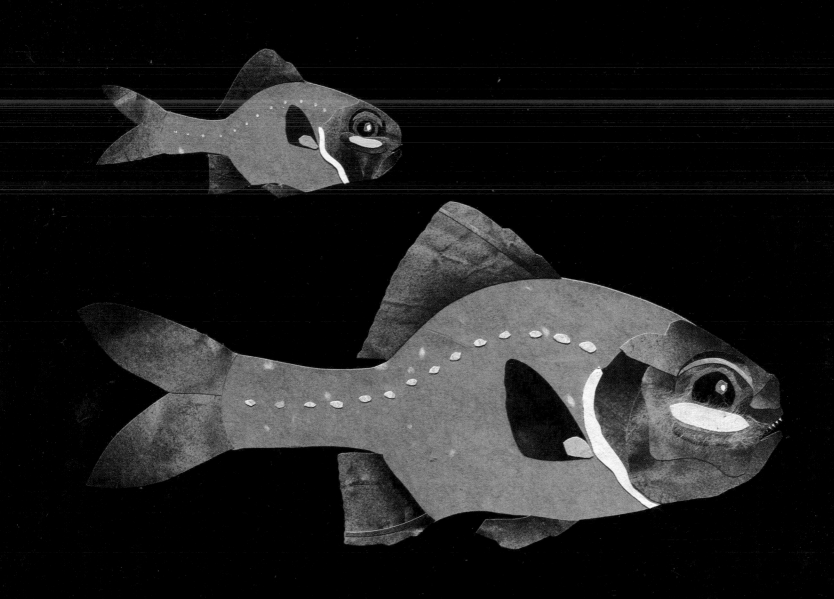

Flashlight fish live deep in the ocean, where it's always dark. They have a bright glowing spot under each eye that they can cover and uncover with a flap of skin. The flashes are used to communicate with other flashlight fish and to confuse predators.

Elephants make a growling sound with their stomachs, too low for humans to hear, that can be heard by other elephants miles away. These sounds help the members of their group stay together.

Bats make a continuous and very high pitched series of squeaks as they fly. These sounds bounce off of nearby objects and allow the bat to communicate and to fly in total darkness. A mother bat returning to her cave gives a special cry and listens for an answering call so she can locate her baby among two or three million other young bats.

Some animals are able to tell one another where food is located by using visual signals or chemical signals.

Turkey vultures circle above dead or dying animals they spot on the ground. When other vultures see this, they join in. Finally, the large group of birds lands together. This way, they have a better chance of frightening off competing scavengers.

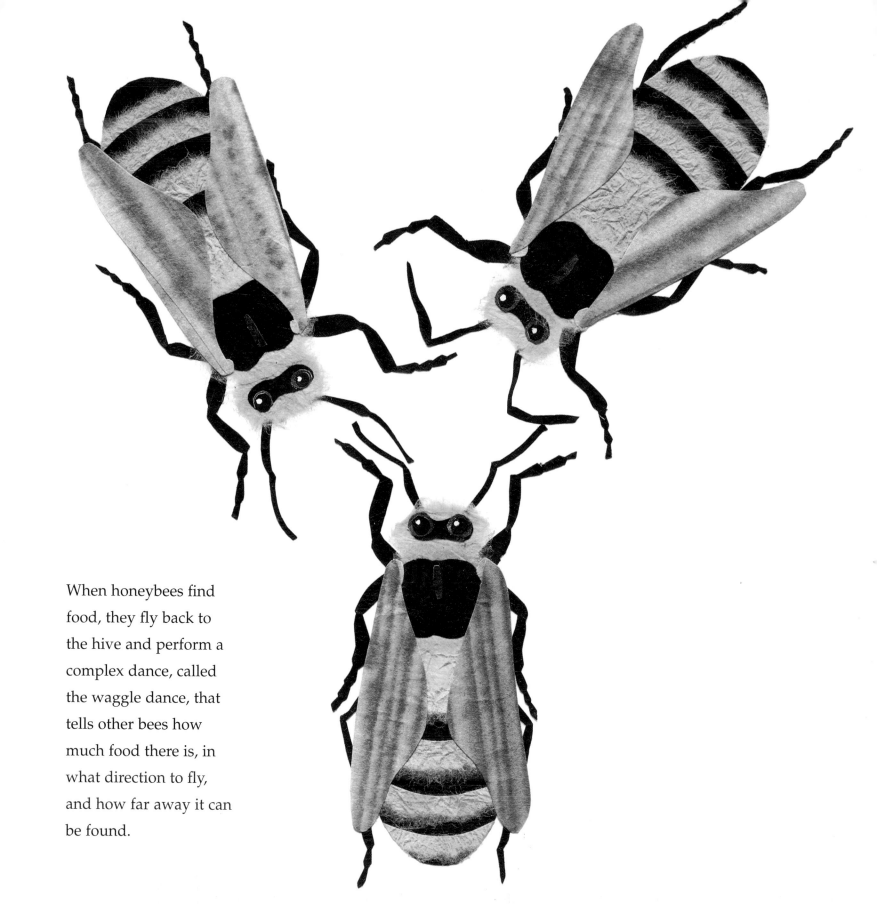

When honeybees find food, they fly back to the hive and perform a complex dance, called the waggle dance, that tells other bees how much food there is, in what direction to fly, and how far away it can be found.

When it finds food, the fire ant makes a chemical trail for other ants to follow by touching the tip of its tail to the ground at regular intervals.

Certain animals are territorial — they claim a particular piece of land or property as their own and defend it against others of their kind. They need to be able to let other animals know that "this belongs to me."

The klipspringer antelope has a special scent gland on its face. It pushes against twigs or branches with this gland, leaving its scent on trees or bushes. The scent marks its territory for other klipspringers.

When a house cat rubs its head against its owner's legs, it isn't showing affection. A special scent gland on the cat's head leaves an odor that tells other cats that this human belongs to it.

The male hippopotamus scatters its dung with its tail, which spins like a propeller. The hippo uses this unusual technique to let other hippos know that this is his territory.

For Jamie, Alec, and Page

Bibliography

Bailey, Jill. *Animal Life.*
New York: Oxford University Press, 1994.

Caras, Roger. *The Private Lives of Animals.*
New York: Grosset & Dunlap Publishers, 1974.

Casale, Paolo. *Animal Behavior.*
Florence, Italy: Barron's Educational Series, 1999.

Facklam, Margery. *Bees Dance and Whales Sing.*
San Francisco: Sierra Books for Children, 1992.

Gould, Dr. Edwin, and Dr. George McKay, eds. *Encyclopedia of Mammals.*
2nd edition. San Diego: Academic Press, 1998.

Wyckoff, Betsy. *Talking Apes & Dancing Bees.*
Barrytown, New York: Station Hill/Barrytown, 1999.

Copyright © 2001 by Steve Jenkins

www.houghtonmifflinbooks.com

The text of this book is set in Palatino.
The section introductions are set in Franklin Gothic Condensed.
The illustrations are collages of cut and torn paper.

Library of Congress Cataloging-in-Publication Data

Jenkins, Steve, 1952–.
Slap, squeak, and scatter : how animals communicate / written and illustrated by Steve Jenkins.
p. cm.
ISBN 0-618-03376-9
1. Animal communication — Juvenile literature. [1. Animal communication.] I. Title.
QL776.J46 2001   591.59 — dc21   00-061402

Manufactured in the United States of America
BVG 10 9 8 7 6 5 4 3 2 1